The Extended Curriculum

Meeting the Needs of Young People

Books are to be returned on or before
the last date below.

Matthew Griffiths

Carol Tennyson

David Fulton Publishers

London

28055

David Fulton Publishers Ltd
Ormond House, 26–27 Boswell Street, London WC1N 3JD

First published in Great Britain by David Fulton Publishers 1997

Note: The right of Matthew Griffiths and Carol Tennyson to be identified as the authors of this work has been asserted by them in accordance with the Copyright, Designs and Patents Act 1988.

Copyright © Matthew Griffiths and Carol Tennyson 1997

British Library Cataloguing in Publication Data
A catalogue record for this book is available from the British Library

ISBN 1–85346–433–3

All rights reserved. The materials in this publication may be photocopied for use only within the purchasing organisation.

Typeset by Sheila Knight, London
Printed in Great Britain by Bell and Bain Ltd, Glasgow

Contents

Preface

The publication of this workbook coincides with the end of the consultation period on 'Inclusive Learning', the report of the findings and recommendations of the Learning Difficulties and/or Disabilities Committee to the Further Education Funding Council (FEFC). The immediate purpose of that report was radically to improve educational opportunities for about 130,000 students with learning difficulties and/or disabilities who are currently attending further education colleges and other centres. This workbook has the same purpose.

In Chapter 2 of 'Inclusive Learning', the committee state that:

> Inclusive learning is a way of thinking about further education that uses a revitalised understanding of learning and the learner's requirements as its starting point . . . . By 'inclusive learning', therefore, we mean the greatest degree of match or fit between the individual learner's requirements and the provision that is made for them.

This workbook aims to enable establishments to develop a curriculum framework and individual programmes which provide that degree of match between the learner's requirement and the provision made.

'Inclusive Learning' has generated more responses than any other consultation document which the Council has published. Many colleges, both within the FEFC sector and outside it, will want to develop ways of meeting students' needs by matching them with the provision made. This workbook, if used effectively, will enable colleges, including specialist residential colleges, to develop inclusive learning. It is about an honest audit of the learners' needs and the provision available, and about bringing the two together to enable the students to make the best possible progress in their learning.

Like the concepts described in 'Inclusive Learning', the concepts set out in this book are deceptively simple at first sight. They require, however, considerable hard work and expertise if they are to be to be translated successfully into practice. It will not be easy for any staff group to work through this book. They will need effective leadership, honesty, perseverance, tenacity and concentration. Groups can only sustain this with the support of senior managers. The results can, however, be spectacular. Students whose learning needs have been matched by individual programmes, set within an appropriate curriculum framework, can learn effectively, sometimes for the first time. Staff groups which can achieve this will feel that the effort was worthwhile.

Introduction

The original idea for this book came from a need for guidance for residential colleges in designing an extended curriculum for students with disabilities. However, as it is based on the principles of good curriculum design, it can be used equally effectively to design a curriculum framework for a conventional college day. It could also be used as a basis for post-16 provision in schools, provision in social education centres or any other establishment offering education.

A curriculum for residential education

Residential provision is expensive. Current thinking on good practice in education also focuses on the right of children, young people and adults to attend their local schools and colleges. Those who provide residential education now have to prove that what they offer is good value for money. They also need to show that they provide something which could not be replicated in a day provision. The value of residential further education, both to the students and the funding body, lies in the extended curriculum. The extended curriculum enables residential establishments to capitalise on the unique area of their provision – the fact that students have the residential accommodation, and an extended day, in which to learn.

Learning can and does take place anywhere at any time. However, education puts learning within a formal curriculum framework. This requires the ordering of activities to enhance opportunities for learning in pre-selected areas. In an educational setting, a curriculum framework sets out the areas in which learning will take place, together with the chosen methods, staffing and settings which should give learners the best opportunities to learn. Learning is therefore maximised. The lack of a developed curriculum framework is the most major and the most frequently reported weakness identified by inspectors. Many establishments are new to curriculum development and have great difficulty in designing a framework for learning and individual programmes to meet students' specific needs and aspirations.

Who is this workbook for?

This workbook is for staff teams who want to develop a framework for learning within which individual programmes can be designed to meet students' specific needs. In most colleges and schools this will be the teaching staff and their immediate managers.

Most residential colleges and schools, however, have two main teams of staff; those who provide education and those who provide care. The structure is just like that of a day school or college, except that the care is not provided by the student's own family. Often the two teams are separate and come together only in the principal or head teacher's post. Members may have little contact with each other. The extended curriculum is based on the assumption that all staff in an educational establishment have a role in helping the students to learn. All members of both staff teams will have a part to play. Everyone needs to understand the concept of the extended curriculum and how they can each contribute to learning. For those using this workbook in a day setting, the 'care team' may be the students' own families or the staff of the home where they live. Or you may decide that you are able to deliver aspects of the extended curriculum either within the existing day timetable, or by extending it into the evening on one or more days of the week.

How can this workbook be used?

The workbook is designed to be used for real curriculum change. Staff work through the sessions to build up a new or more finely-tuned curriculum framework, and individually tailored programmes for all the students. As this is the core area of any educational establishment's existence, everyone needs to be involved in it. Ideally the earlier work sessions should involve all staff, or representatives of all staff groups. These sessions are about what the students need, and what the college can offer to meet their educational needs. Considerable emphasis is placed on the different roles of all staff in meeting the full range of needs. Other sessions are more appropriate for groups of managers, teaching staff and care staff or parents and carers.

All sessions indicate which groups might most usefully be involved, but different systems and professional structures in some establishments may require different attendance in sessions. As the workbook focuses on professional curriculum development, any group using it will need to include at least one trained and qualified teacher, who has an understanding of curriculum development. Establishments which do not have trained teachers on the staff may wish to engage a consultant to lead the group, or use the expertise of someone associated with the college. It is vital, however, that the staff do work through the process, and do not have it carried out on their behalf. If staff are not involved in the process, they will not be able to work effectively within it.

The book is structured so that the staff group will work logically through the process of building up the structure for the whole provision, and then work on the individual programmes for the students. It is important that the whole process is covered. Colleges should consider working through the whole process about once every four or five years so that staff can reconsider the provision in the light of any changes which have taken place. Changes in the student group, the staff and the college facilities all need to be considered in subsequent reviews.

You may also wish to use the workbook for staff induction or training, when the activities will be carried out as exercises rather than in reality.

The work sessions have been written to cover individual elements of curriculum development. In some sessions the contents are complex or time-consuming. They may need to be broken down into two or more sessions. It will always be more productive to split a session than to overload it.

Before you begin you might wish to study the following diagram which illustrates the process of developing individual programmes within the framework of the extended curriculum.

DEVELOPING INDIVIDUAL PROGRAMMES WITHIN THE EXTENDED CURRICULUM

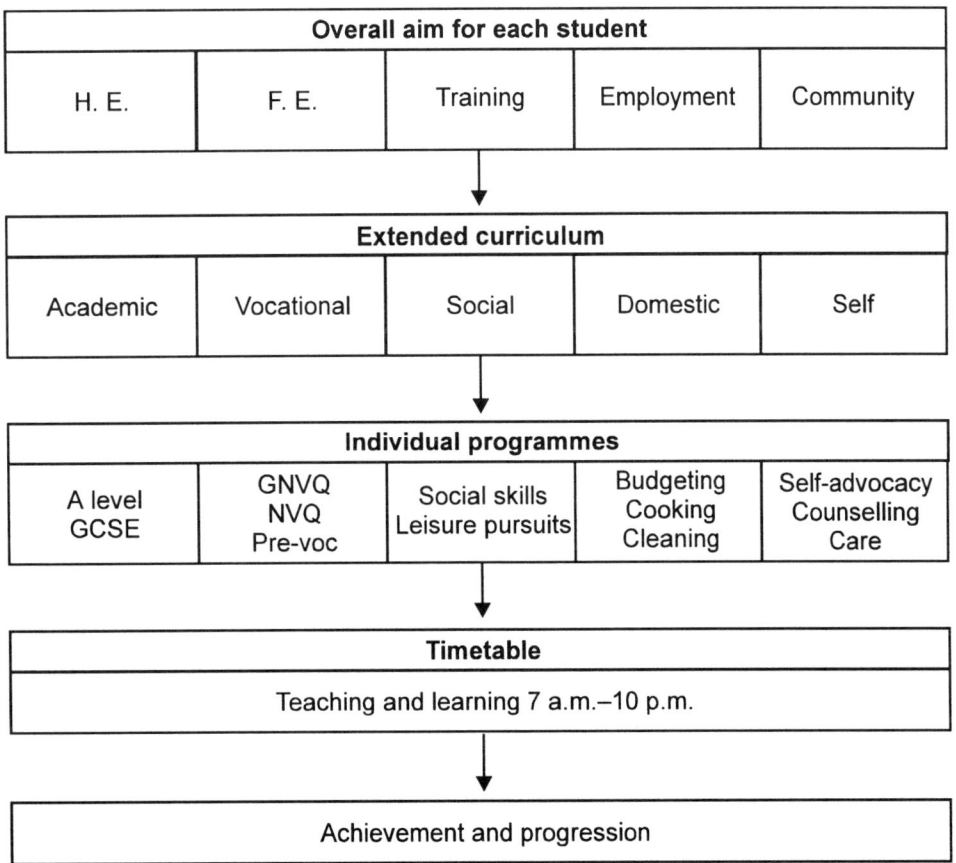

H. E.	Higher education
F. E.	Further education
A level	Advanced level
GCSE	General Certificate of Secondary Education
GNVQ	General National Vocational Qualification
NVQ	National Vocational Qualification

Part 1

The Framework for Learning: the Courses

The Students and their Learning Needs

(Whole staff)

To decide what kinds of courses you need to offer, you need first to look very carefully at the students who come to you now, and those who are likely to come in the near future. They may or may not be the same as those who came a few years ago. Mainstream schools and colleges are increasingly responding to the challenge of meeting the educational needs of children, young people and adults with disabilities. In many cases, this means that students for whom residential education is now sought will have more complex difficulties or other difficulties in their lives. You will need to be particularly clear about the real needs of these students if you are to meet them successfully.

Activity 1

Brainstorm

Who are the students?

- What are their characteristics?
- What is their range of disabilities?
- Are they within one age group, or can their ages be very different?
- Are they different from the students who came a few years ago, or are they likely to be a different group in the future?

Activity 2

Small group discussion with conclusions presented to the whole group and retained for typing up

Who are the students?

Groups pick out the most important characteristics of the student group from the brainstorm record sheet.

Activity 3

Small group discussion

What do they need to learn?

Given the key characteristics of the students, what do they need to learn? In order to carry out this exercise successfully, you need to have a clear picture of what their lives are like now, and what they will be like in the future. What are the priorities? Remember that, although the students may have numerous gaps in their learning, you will only have them for two or three years. What are the things which will really make a difference, even if they do not progress in the others?

If several different groups of students have been identified, it may be useful to have a different small group work on each one. Different groups may be those such as immature school-leavers with few self-care skills; newly disabled adults; those with complex disabilities; those preparing for higher education; those preparing for living in group homes.

To help you take the work forward you now already have:

- a picture of the student group(s) for whom education will be offered
- a picture of their general learning needs.

Use the picture of the students' general learning needs to select the elements which need to be included in the curriculum.

Example

The brainstorm: who are the students?

Young people with a wide range of ability and hearing loss. Between 16 and 22 years old.

All students have profound, severe or partial hearing loss. In addition students may also have:

- moderate learning difficulties

- severe learning difficulties

- some physical disability

- emotional and behavioural difficulties

- visual impairment

- mental health problems.

Some students have a combination of difficulties.

All students learn through total communication which includes signing, speech, lip-reading, gesture and facial expression.

Used to be more students who did not have learning difficulties; more students now have a cluster of disabilities.

Most have spent most or a large part of their school days in residential education. Less mature than others of their age. Likely to have little experience of having to cope as adults in a hearing world where total communication does not operate.

Small group discussion: key characteristics of the student group

- Different groups have different needs.

- All, except possibly the most severely intellectually impaired, need to be able to cope with hearing people and the hearing world.

- Most need domestic skills and to learn to look after themselves.

- Most need to 'grow up'.

- There are not so many students who can benefit from GCSE or A level courses as previously – more need pre-foundation level courses.

Small group discussion: what do they need to learn?

- Need for a range of different courses

- Need for specific elements of all students' courses to focus on communicating with hearing people

- Need for specific elements of all students' courses to focus on domestic skills and looking after oneself

- Need for specific elements of all students' courses to focus on adulthood and adult responsibilities

- Need for a growth in pre-foundation courses.

Where are you now?

At the end of this session the group will have built up a clear picture of the students who are currently enrolled, and of what they need to learn to have most opportunities in their future lives.

Notes

Work session 2

The Extended Curriculum

(Whole staff)

From the previous session, you will have a clear general picture of who your students are, and what they need to learn. In this session you will be working on how the things they need to learn will take place within an extended curriculum.

The extended curriculum removes the boundary between the traditional timetabled part of the day (usually between 9 a.m. and 4 p.m. or similar times) and the rest of the day.

This means that the time used for students to learn extends significantly beyond the typical college or school day. Planned, timetabled learning takes place at any appropriate time to meet the students' particular needs and achieve their goals. This does not mean that all activities are formal 'lessons', even though goals and content are carefully planned. The student should not feel that everything is a classroom activity!

Activity 1

Whole group discussion

Why do your students need an extended curriculum?

From your previous session you will have:

- a picture of the student group(s) to whom education is offered in your establishment
- a picture of their general learning needs.

Use it to determine why these learning needs cannot be met within a traditionally timetabled college or school day.

Activity 2

Small group activity

Where and when should they learn?

Using the list you drew up of what your students need to learn, decide which aspects could best be taught in which parts of the day.

Waking to 9 a.m.	
9 a.m. to lunchtime	
Lunchtime	
End of lunchtime to 4 p.m.	
4 p.m. to bedtime	

Activity 3

Whole staff

Where and when should they learn?

Bring the time allocations of the small groups together and use them to make one overall chart which sets out the times when staff and students will focus on different kinds of activities.

Example

Why do your students need an extended curriculum?

- They need to learn so many things.

- They need to learn things which you can only teach in a home or residential unit, not in a classroom.

- They're only here for two or three years so we have to make use of all the time available.

- Residential education is so expensive and we have to give value for money if funding bodies are going to continue to send us students.

- The inspectorate look for it and it is part of what they grade.

- So that the students can get the most benefit from their time here.

Example for more able students

Where and when should they learn?

Waking to 9 a.m.	personal care skills/domestic skills
9 a.m. to lunchtime	courses
Lunchtime	personal care skills/domestic skills
End of lunchtime to 4 p.m.	courses
4 p.m. to bedtime	personal care skills/domestic skills/skills for leisure

Example for students with more severe learning difficulties

Where and when should they learn?

Waking to 9 a.m.	personal care skills/domestic skills
9 a.m. to lunchtime	personal care skills/domestic skills
Lunchtime	personal care skills/domestic skills
End of lunchtime to 4 p.m.	personal development (communication/numeracy/ making sense of the world)
4 p.m. to bedtime	personal care skills/domestic skills/skills for leisure

If you are working in a day provision, or have some students who attend on a daily basis you will wish to discuss with the parents or carers how they could contribute to the extended curriculum. You may also wish to discuss the way forward if you feel that you cannot offer an extended curriculum. The whole of the rest of the workbook will still be relevant, but you will need to have a view on what range of needs can realistically be met in the time that you and the students have available.

Notes

Work session 3

The Establishment and its Aims

(Whole staff)

You will now have working statements about the students, their needs and the different patterns of the day which could enable you to meet their needs through an extended curriculum. You will have decided what kinds of courses you need to offer to meet their needs. Now you need to examine the way your establishment operates and the constraints under which you have to work. You are thinking about using all aspects of the establishment for learning but you also need to be honest and realistic about what it cannot provide.

This work session can be particularly demanding. You may wish to spread it over two sessions.

Activity 1

Whole group discussion

Setting the mission statement

What is your educational mission? Agree a clear and concise mission statement which sets out what you are aiming to achieve. If your establishment works on the basis of religious, philosophical or other beliefs, you should ensure that this is explicit, as this will be a fundamental part of what you do (see the following page for examples of mission statements).

Examples

Mission statements

- To provide a safe, nurturing and empowering environment in which young people with learning difficulties and associated behavioural, emotional and/or social difficulties, can confidently complete the transition from adolescence into the adult world.

- To provide a total residential learning experience for young people who are profoundly prelingually deaf, with associated learning, communication and behavioural disturbance.

- To provide further education and employment training for people with autism and related conditions.

- To work closely with FEFC sector colleges to provide: vocational, social and functional integration; skills for living independently in the community; and the skills and confidence to enable visually impaired people to gain and retain employment.

The aims for different groups of students:

- To enable some students to gain entry to higher education; to equip them with the skills to live in student accommodation; and to give them the social skills and confidence to enjoy the student experience.

- To enable some students to gain entry to higher level courses in colleges of further education; to equip them to live more independently; and to give them the social skills and confidence to enjoy the student experience.

- To enable some students to gain entry to employment; to equip them to live more independently; and to give them the social skills and confidence to maintain employment.

- To enable some students to gain entry to further training for employment; to equip them to live more independently; and to give them the social skills and confidence to succeed in their training.

- To enable some students live more independently; and to give them the social skills and confidence to enjoy a range of activities and participate in them effectively.

- To enable some students to communicate and receive communication at a basic level so that they can take a more active part in their own lives.

Activity 2

Small group discussion

Setting the aims for different groups of students

Once you have agreed the overall mission statement, use small group discussions to agree how the mission will be interpreted for different groups of students.

Activity 3

Small group discussion

Identifying conflicting aims

Clarify the nature of any aims which the establishment has in addition to its educational aims. For example, the provision of care; the desire to meet parents' wishes; the provision of an alternative to family life for children or young people; the need to register as a care home; or the requirements of funders who are purchasing non-educational provision. How could these aims conflict with the educational aims? How can such conflicts be minimised? If they are very significant, what can be done?

Activity 4

Brainstorm

Aims we meet (strengths) and those we do not (weaknesses)

Brainstorm the ways in which the educational aims for different students are already met in your existing curriculum. Which aims are not achieved or are only partially achieved?

What needs to be done to make the strengths even stronger, and to address the weaknesses?

Where are you now?

At the end of this session all staff will be clear about the educational mission, its different interpretation for different students, the possibility of conflicting aims and the strengths and weaknesses in the achievement of the aims. (Allow sufficient – possibly extra – structured discussion to ensure that this shared level of understanding has been reached.)

Notes

Strengths and Constraints

(Whole staff)

To check what you can realistically offer, you need to audit the strengths and weaknesses of your accommodation, equipment and staff qualifications and experience against the elements of the provision you plan to offer. Throughout this workbook the curriculum will be divided into the five elements shown in the table below.

Academic	Vocational	Social	Domestic	Self
A Levels GCSE	GNVQ NVQ	Leisure interests and activities	Living independently Shopping Cleaning Cooking Being involved in routines	Awareness of self Confidence Relating to others Rules of behaviour

This work session can be particularly time-consuming. You may wish to spread it over two sessions.

Activity 1

Small group exercise

Accommodation

Take each element of the curriculum (i.e. academic, vocational, social, domestic, self) and decide what accommodation you have which would provide a good quality environment for teaching in that area.

Academic	Vocational	Social	Domestic	Self

Activity 2

Whole group exercise

Accommodation

Bring together the small group decisions and agree a whole-establishment view of the relevance of all aspects of accommodation to the requirements of students' learning. How can different rooms, outside areas, or other facilities be used to enable students to learn? Are there any aspects of teaching for which accommodation is poor or inappropriate? What should happen as a result of this judgement? (Improve the accommodation or discontinue the activity?) Don't forget the residential accommodation. Is it well designed to help students learn? Does the layout of the accommodation enable students to learn to live more independently as their skills for independent living increase?

Examples

Analysis of the use of residential accommodation

- At a college for profoundly prelingually deaf students, living skills are an important and well developed area of the curriculum. Students make considerable progress through a modular course, which is linked to progress through four levels of residential accommodation. New students have single bedrooms. Their washing is done for them, all meals are provided and they are supervised carefully in self-care and leisure activities. When they have passed the required number of modules on the course, they move into bedsitting rooms and do more for themselves. They can then progress to a flat and ultimately to independent living in a house in the college grounds. Every student has a key worker who supports and helps them at every stage.

- In another setting, students progress through three houses which are run differently to enable students to move into accommodation with less support as their skills develop. In the house where the most independent students live, they prepare their own breakfast and supper on most days and share in the preparation of more formal meals at weekends when the group eat together. These students purchase food locally and care for the house jointly.

Activity 3

Small group exercise

Equipment

Take each element of the curriculum and decide what equipment you have which would provide a good quality support for teaching.

Academic	Vocational	Social	Domestic	Self

Activity 4

Whole group exercise

Equipment

Bring together the small group decisions and agree a whole-establishment view of the relevance of all aspects of equipment to the requirements of students' learning. Are there any aspects of teaching for which equipment is poor or inappropriate? Again, what should happen as a result of this judgement? (Improve the equipment or discontinue the activity?) Don't forget the residential accommodation. Is it well equipped to help students learn? Does the way in which the residential accommodation is equipped enable students to learn to live more independently as their skills for independent living increase?

Examples

Analysis of equipment

- Because of the degree of students' physical disabilities all kitchens are equipped with microwave ovens to enable as many students as possible to cook independently.

- The A level art course is no longer offered in the college because the art room was not properly equipped to enable it to be taught effectively. It would be unrealistic to purchase the necessary range of equipment for the small numbers of students who require the course. Students who want to take A level art are now supported at the local sector college.

- Students use a brickwork shop which is fully equipped for NVQs in brickwork. It provides a simulated work environment. Students use the equipment efficiently and effectively.

Activity 5

Small group exercise

Staff qualifications and experience

Take each element of the curriculum and decide what qualifications and experience staff have which would enable them to provide quality teaching.

Academic	Vocational	Social	Domestic	Self

Activity 6

Whole staff

Staff qualifications and experience

Bring together the small group decisions and agree a whole-establishment view of the relevance of all aspects of staff qualifications and experience to the requirements of students' learning. Are there any aspects of teaching for which staff qualifications and experience are poor or inappropriate? Again, what should happen as a result of this judgement? (Change or reskill staff or discontinue the activity?) Don't forget the residential accommodation. Is it appropriately staffed to help students learn? Does the way in which the residential accommodation is staffed enable students to learn to live more independently as their skills for independent living increase?

Examples

Analysis of staffing skills

- There is careful individual teaching in which students have full personal attention. A variety of teaching strategies is used to enable them to learn. Staff relate to students warmly and supportively, in a manner appropriate to both their ages and their levels of understanding. However, because of poor organisation of groups, some students wait for long periods, or receive hurried support or divided attention. Some undirected use of classroom assistants contributes to this.

- A member of staff whose qualifications are City and Guilds' Heating and Ventilation Engineering Craft; Oxyacetylene Welding Advanced Craft; Metal-Arc Welding; and Plumbing Craft has teaching responsibilities which include: catering; domestic skills; numeracy, literacy; retail and distribution; communication; and painting and decorating.

Sometimes changes are made at the same time in more than one area to bring about the developments which the establishment needs. For example in one residential college changes in accommodation, equipment, staffing and staff skills have been carried out to enable a new curriculum, more appropriate to the needs of the students, to operate successfully. A former classroom has been divided, and converted into a horticulture storage and preparation area, and an animal care area. A building previously used for storage has been converted to a small animal house, with an aviary built on to the side. A number of rabbits, rats, guinea pigs, stick insects and birds have been acquired. The unit where the most independent students now live has a newly converted kitchen and dining-area. New computer and software packages have been purchased. A teacher with experience of students with learning difficulties has been recruited to lead the development of basic skills and IT. Three effective new classroom assistants now support the students in their learning. The creation of a new head of care post allows the more effective development of the residential aspects of the provision. A programme of staff development has been put in place to enhance their skills in the areas required by the new curriculum

Where are you now?

By the end of this session the group will have conducted a thorough audit of the accommodation, equipment and staff expertise in the establishment. This audit will be particularly valuable for the next work session, which examines the constraints under which the establishment operates.

Notes

Work session 5

Constraints

(Whole staff)

No establishment can offer everything. What are the constraints which the current accommodation, equipment and staff expertise place on what can be taught within your establishment? It's never a good idea to offer anything which you can't do well. Good practice involves offering programmes effectively at different levels to enable students to progress from basic level courses to more advanced programmes as their skills and confidence increase. Effective provision can only be made in appropriate accommodation, by skilful staff, with access to the correct equipment. Programmes need to be taught by staff who are skilled in the subject area and knowledgeable about the educational implications of students' disabilities and/or learning difficulties. As such, this provision demands the most skilled and experienced staff, not well-meaning amateurs who simply have an interest in the work. Effective provision is found in those colleges which are realistic about what they can offer and do not attempt to offer programmes for which they do not have the expertise.

Activity 1

Small group discussion

Resources

Are there areas in which it is difficult to offer high quality teaching because of lack of appropriate accommodation, equipment or staff expertise?

Academic	Vocational	Social	Domestic	Self

Are there any areas in which it is no longer appropriate to offer provision because of changes in the student group?

Activity 2

Whole group activity

Resources (continued)

Examine the responses to Activity 1 and reach an overall view as to whether accommodation, equipment or staff expertise will be improved in areas which have been identified as weak, or whether areas on current offer will be changed or discontinued. Who will take forward these views?

Where are you now?

By the end of this activity, the group will have built the foundations for the construction of a unique, appropriate curriculum offer for the establishment. This is a significant achievement. Take some time to review all the work to date and to set out the elements which have been identified as vital in curriculum construction.

Notes

Planning the Construction of the Extended Curriculum

(Teaching staff)

You now have the background information which will enable you to construct the right extended curriculum for the students you have and in the setting in which you work.

The delivery of the curriculum involves all staff. All staff are involved in helping students to learn. However, development of the curriculum is led by teachers, who are the educational experts with the training and experience to lead in this work. As you will be focusing on professional curriculum development, the group will need to include at least one trained and qualified teacher, who has an understanding of curriculum development. If you do not have trained teachers on the staff, you should consider engaging a consultant to lead the group, or use the expertise of someone associated with the college. It is vital, however, that the staff do work through the process, and do not have it carried out on their behalf. If staff are not involved in the process, they will not be able to work effectively within it. The development of the curriculum is likely to be most successful when senior managers endorse, manage, understand and contribute to the process. Governors and advisory committees can also help the development of the extended curriculum by getting to understand the concept and endorsing and confirming their allegiance to it.

Provision is most successful in colleges where senior managers provide strong, effective leadership, are knowledgeable about the work, committed to developing an inclusive approach to education in which all students are perceived to be of equal value, and demand the same level of rigour as they do for any other area of provision. A policy which has been developed by staff from across the college articulates the college's philosophy in relation to its provision for students with disabilities and/or learning difficulties and provides a framework for the development of the provision. Care is taken to ensure that the provision is coordinated across the college. This entails establishing clear roles and responsibilities, identifying people for each aspect of the college's work and providing sufficient time for the coordination of the provision.

Activity 1

All teaching staff

Establishing your working group

Decide who will be part of the group to take the lead in constructing the curriculum. Members of the group should:

- be enthusiastic and committed to the concept
- have sufficient time to contribute effectively
- be able to meet regularly at an agreed time
- represent all the areas in which the curriculum will be developed
- be able to be open and honest about the establishment and its work.

Activity 2

All teaching staff

Establishing a framework and timescale

Decide in advance exactly how the group will operate. You will need to agree:

- a realistic timescale for the process (probably an academic year)
- dates for the presentation of position papers and interim reports
- a format within which everyone will work
- ways of involving those not in the group, when this is appropriate.

Activity 3

Teaching staff working group

Managing the process and keeping on task

Agree a chairperson for the group whose main role will be to manage the process and keep the group on task.

Activity 4

Teaching staff working group

Introducing the extended curriculum

Agree at this point, before detailed work begins, how changes and developments in the curriculum will be managed and how changes will be introduced to students, parents and outside agencies. As the whole staff group will have been involved in the earlier sessions, everyone will already have been part of discussions and decisions. They will still need, however, to be kept up to date on developments.

Where are you now?

At the end of this session the group will have set up a process which will enable an extended curriculum to be developed effectively for their specific student group in their particular establishment.

Notes

Construction of the Extended Curriculum

(Teaching staff working group; senior staff and governors)

As was shown in Work session 4, the following elements can be seen as the major areas of learning which will be encompassed in the extended curriculum. They are the areas in which students need to learn, if they are to progress successfully into adult life. Academically able students still need to learn across these areas, so ensure that they are considered for all students.

Academic	Vocational	Social	Domestic	Self
A Levels GCSE	GNVQ NVQ Pre-vocational training	Leisure interests and activities	Living independently Shopping Cleaning Cooking Being involved in routines	Awareness of self Confidence Relating to others Rules of behaviour

These elements will form the basis of all students' individual learning programmes. During the following work session you will be setting up the contents of the areas within which these programmes will be planned.

THIS IS ONE OF THE KEY SECTIONS IN THE CONSTRUCTION OF THE CURRICULUM. TAKE AS LONG OVER IT AS NECESSARY.

As you decide on the key elements of the curriculum, you will need to think carefully about accreditation, and how it will enhance the students' opportunities to move on to other things. The lack of formal recognition and evidence of students' achievements can be a major weakness in both non-sector and FEFC colleges. At present there is no general framework for the accreditation of courses leading to NVQ 1 and GNVQ Foundation. This can cause real difficulties when setting up or evaluating progression routes between the multiplicity of qualifications available. Students may move between different pre-vocational programmes, all of which are externally accredited, with no clear progression route. If your provision includes students with very severe disabilities, you will also need to decide how you will produce properly recorded evidence of their achievements and progress, often in areas of learning or at levels of development which are outside the parameters of external accreditation. The group will need to decide on appropriate accreditation for pre-vocational programmes, if it is thought to be useful for students. Think carefully about accreditation for the other curriculum areas. Use accreditation when it is useful for progression.

Activity 1

Teaching staff working group

What academic courses will be on offer?

The group should agree:

- which academic courses the students need and want

- whether there are courses which students may want, but which staff feel inappropriate

- whether there are courses for which you do not have the staff expertise, accommodation or equipment to offer on site

- whether group sizes are viable and appropriate (many subjects are best taught in groups which allow for discussion, different points of view and small group projects)

- which courses are available at a local college of further education, where students could be taught with support

- whether GCSE retakes should be offered (few students gain a significantly higher grade when they retake GCSE examinations – if students are to retake any examination they should have a specific reason for needing the subject at an A–C grade and a realistic chance of achieving this

- whether A levels are a realistic option.

Activity 2

Teaching staff working group

What vocational courses will be on offer?

The group should agree:

- the range of vocational subjects which can be taught (depending on the staff and facilities available or capable of being developed)

- the range of levels which should be available (pre-foundation, foundation, intermediate, advanced)

- whether intermediate and advanced level GNVQs should be offered as an alternative to GCSE and A levels

- whether NVQs, for which a real work environment is needed, are to be offered

- which courses are available at a local college of further education, where students could be taught with support

- how work experience will be developed to contribute to vocational teaching and learning

- how students who need it will be prepared for and introduced to sheltered employment

- what accreditation will be used.

Activity 3

Teaching staff working group

What will be on offer to enable students to learn through social and leisure activities?

The group should agree:

- how a programme of social and leisure activities will be organised as part of students' opportunities

- how students' differing needs for developing skills in this area will be assessed

- how information will be gathered as to particular requirements of students' future settings such as higher education, specific residential communities, employment in a non-disabled setting, or life within a group home

- who will teach the students

- how learning will be planned, recorded and evaluated

- how evidence of achievement will be gathered and whether accreditation will be used.

Activity 4

Teaching staff working group

What will be on offer to enable students to learn domestic skills for their adult lives?

The group should agree:

- how a programme of domestic activities will be organised as part of students' opportunities

- how students' differing needs for developing skills in this area will be assessed

- how information will be gathered as to particular requirements of students' future settings such as higher education, specific residential communities, employment in a non-disabled setting, or life within a group home

- who will teach the students

- how learning will be planned, recorded and evaluated

- how evidence of achievement will be gathered and whether accreditation will be used.

Activity 5

Teaching staff working group

What will be on offer to enable students to develop the skills to operate more successfully in their adult lives?

The group should agree:

- how a programme of self-development will be organised as part of students' opportunities

- how students' differing needs for developing skills in this area will be assessed

- how information will be gathered as to particular requirements of students' future settings such as higher education, specific residential communities, employment in a non-disabled setting, or life within a group home

- who will teach the students

- who or what will ensure that all staff, in all activities, contribute to students' development as competent and confident adults

- how learning will be planned, recorded and evaluated

- how evidence of achievement will be gathered and whether accreditation will be used.

Where are you now?

By the end of this section of the workbook, staff will have planned the major areas of the curriculum, in readiness for the development of students' individual learning programmes.

The group will know what each of the curriculum areas might contain and how each will be coherent within itself and with all other areas.

Activity 6

Discussion: senior staff and governors

The role of senior staff and governors

Senior staff and governors should establish:

- how they will respond to the new curriculum

- how they will receive the information about it and how they will respond

- what mechanisms they need for the implementation of changes which are needed as the result of the development.

Notes

Work session 8

Delivery

(Teaching staff working group)

Now that all the areas of the curriculum framework have been mapped out, the group should consider how the framework will be fleshed out. Who will do what, where, when and how?

Activity 1

Either the whole working group considers each group of students or the working group divides into groups, each considering one student group

Timetables

For each group of students set out a proposed timetable for all five areas of the timetable (see opposite). Begin to plan who will teach in each area, according to their experience and expertise.

Timetables will need to be compatible for different groups to ensure that there are no accommodation or staff clashes.

In the second part of the workbook, planning will move on to what individual students will be doing in each session.

Notes

Example

Timetable

Monday	Academic	Vocational	Social	Domestic	Self development
7–9 a.m.					
9–12 p.m.					
12–1 p.m.					
1–3 p.m.					
3–5 p.m.					
5–8 p.m.					
8–10 p.m.					

Work session 9

Monitoring

(Teaching staff working group; senior staff and governors)

Curriculum development is never a single activity. The curriculum on offer needs to be reviewed each year to establish whether:

- the curriculum is still appropriate for students' needs and realistic aspirations
- staff, accommodation and equipment are still effective
- accreditation frameworks are still appropriate
- the balance of the activities can and should be maintained
- changes should be made.

Activity 1

Teaching staff working group

Annual curriculum reviews

The group should establish:

- an annual curriculum review procedure
- the format and content of that review
- the mechanisms for the implementation of changes which are needed as the result of the review.

Activity 2

Senior staff and governors

The role of senior staff and governors

Senior staff and governors should establish:

- how they will ensure that the review takes place

- how they will receive the information generated from the review

- what mechanisms they need for the implementation of changes which are needed as the result of the review.

Where are you now?

The group has the information necessary to set up a system for monitoring the effectiveness of the curriculum areas and is able to ensure that this system operates efficiently.

Notes

Work session 10

Evaluation

(Teaching staff working group; senior staff and governors)

What are the criteria for success? How will you know if the curriculum framework is appropriate? Who will help you decide?

Activity 1

Teaching staff working group

Who will contribute?

List the individuals or groups whose opinions could contribute to the evaluation of the curriculum framework.

Example

Those who could contribute to the evaluation of the curriculum framework

- students
- staff
- former students
- work experience providers
- those who provide for the next phase of students' lives and have received former students
- parents

Activity 2

Teaching staff working group

Curriculum questionnaires

Devise a series of questionnaires for different groups to enable them to contribute their views on the effectiveness of the curriculum you offer, from their perspective.

Activity 3

Teaching staff working group

How to move on

The group should establish:

- how they will ensure that the evaluation takes place
- how they will receive the information generated from the questionnaires
- what mechanisms they need for the implementation of changes which are needed as the result of the evaluation
- how the students' results will contribute to the evaluation.

Activity 4

Senior staff and governors

How to move on

Senior staff and governors should establish:

- how they will ensure that the evaluation takes place
- how they will receive the information generated from the evaluation
- what mechanisms they need for the implementation of changes which are needed as the result of the evaluation.

Where are you now?

You have the information necessary to set up a system for monitoring the effectiveness of the curriculum and ensuring that it runs smoothly.

You have now completed the framework within which all the students will learn every aspect of the curriculum. The second part of the workbook will focus on the design of students' individual learning programmes within this framework.

Notes

Part 2

Using the Framework:
Individual Learning Programmes

Individual Learning Programmes

(Whole staff)

The most essential element of planning individual learning programmes is that they should be based on a realistic assessment of what the students need to learn to prepare them for the next stage of their lives. It has to be accepted that the students will only be funded for a specific period of time and that in order to make the most effective use of this time, staff have to prioritise what they can teach the students in the time available.

It is therefore important that students' individual programmes are developed by setting a goal for the end of their course, assessing their strengths and needs in relation to this goal in order to establish a 'baseline' for their programme, and then developing a programme which will take them from where they are now towards their goal. The programme will include elements of each of the five areas of the extended curriculum.

The following case studies should help you to understand how to identify the learning needs of different students.

Katie is a student at a specialist college for blind students run by a voluntary organisation. She attended mainstream primary and secondary schools where she received support from the peripatetic team for children with visual impairments. She was provided with specialist equipment, including an adapted computer and a variety of low vision aids to help her with practical activities. Both she and her teachers were advised on strategies and teaching methods which would help her to learn effectively. Her vision deteriorated rapidly during her final year in school. This caused her both learning and emotional difficulties which resulted in low grades in all eight of the GCSE examinations for which she had been predicted As and Bs.

Carl was excluded from his comprehensive school when he was 14 for attacking a teacher and breaking his arm. He then attended a school for children with emotional and behavioural difficulties, which he left at 16 without attempting any examinations. He has been assessed as being of slightly above average intellectual ability, with a very poor concentration span, low self-esteem and specific difficulties with reading and spelling. He was arrested as a member of a gang of youths who were caught attempting to set fire to a derelict property. He was cautioned by the police and a place was found for him at a specialist residential further education unit for students with emotional and behavioural difficulties.

Quentin is on a specially designed pre-vocational course at a FEFC sector college. He finds it difficult to understand sentences of more than six words, but can respond to instructions such as 'Give the box to Dilip' , 'Shut the door, please' or 'Put the cup on the table'. Staff have to be careful not to preface instructions to Quentin with introductions such as 'Would you like to . . . ?' or 'Why don't you . . . ?' as this decreases his understanding by extending sentence length beyond his retention. He learns best by copying rather than instruction. He finds it difficult to find his way around without many practice runs. Quentin needs continual reminders that he should not make random comments to strangers or stand or sit too close to people he does not know well. He wants to work in a canteen when he leaves college.

Amy attended a residential special school for pupils with physical disabilities. She was born with cerebral palsy, has little control over her limbs and is totally dependent on others for her personal care. She is unable to speak and uses an electronic communication aid which synthesises speech to communicate with others. Academically she is very able and has six GCSEs at grade C or above. She is not yet certain about her long-term career plans but is keen to pursue her interest in the politics of disability. She now wants to study two A level subjects in the hope that she will be able to go on to higher education.

Activity 1

Brainstorm

What do the students in the case studies need to learn?

What are their strengths?

List the priorities for each student's programme.

Activity 2

Small group exercise

Designing individual programmes

Compare the needs you identified in the previous activity with the ones listed below.

Consider the main elements of the students' individual programmes which have been identified within the five areas of the extended curriculum.

A programme for Katie

Long term aim	higher education
Strengths	determination to succeed
	academically able
	sociable and outgoing personality
	independent in self-care
Needs	academic programme to enable her to gain the qualifications she needs to progress to higher education
	specialist assessment to identify the equipment she needs for her studies
	specialist counselling to help her to work through her difficulties in adjusting to the deterioration in her vision
	mobility training
	specialist careers advice and guidance to help her to identify career options
	a programme to help her to develop the skills she needs to live independently

The main elements of her programme:

Academic	Vocational	Social	Domestic	Self
GCSE	No vocational course	New leisure skills	Skills to live independently at university	New skills to promote confidence and social integration

A programme for Carl	
Long term aim	employment
Strengths	'good with his hands' an interest in cars and motorbikes
Needs	a programme consisting mainly of practical activities work experience specialist counselling to help him to 'manage' his anger 'survival' cookery course basic budgeting / home management skills help to structure his leisure time

The main elements of his programme:

Academic	Vocational	Social	Domestic	Self
No academic course	NVQ 2	New leisure skills	Skills to live independently in a flat	New skills to promote confidence and social integration

A programme for Quentin	
Long term aim	supported employment
Strengths	physical strength and stamina ability to follow simple instructions
Needs	programme to enable him to 'sample' different vocational areas staff who are skilled in giving clear instructions in simple language programme to develop self-care and basic cookery skills programme to develop social skills needed to live with others in a 'group' home

The main elements of his programme:

Academic	Vocational	Social	Domestic	Self
No academic course	Pre-vocational	New leisure skills	Self-care Basic cookery Skills to live in a group home	New skills to promote confidence and social integration

A programme for Amy	
Long term aim	higher education
Strengths	academically able confident and outgoing
Needs	equipment and specialist support to enable her to study the A levels she needs to gain access to higher education help to understand the reality of life at university help to organise carers to provide the support she requires for her personal needs contact with the local coalition of disabled people

The main elements of her programme:

Academic	Vocational	Social	Domestic	Self
A levels	No vocational course	Opportunities to develop new friendships	Skills to live in a hall of residence	New skills to promote confidence and social integration

Activity 3

Small group discussion

Programme amendments

Do you think the proposed programmes are appropriate for the students? List any amendments you would make together with the reasons for the proposed changes.

Activity 4

Paired work (a teacher and a member of the care staff)

Case studies and programmes

Following the examples above, write a brief case study of a student you are currently working with and identify the main elements of an individual programme within the five areas of the curriculum framework to meet the student's needs. Present your work to the rest of the group.

What have you achieved?

You will now have:

- an awareness of the principles underlying the development of individual programmes
- an awareness of the five areas of the curriculum framework
- a detailed picture of the learning needs of a student with whom you are working.

Notes

Work session 12

Implementing the Individual Programmes

(Whole staff)

This work session is lengthy and demanding. You may wish to spread the work over two sessions.

It is important that every member of staff who works with a student is aware of what they are hoping to achieve with the student. Although the choice of subjects or activities is important, it is more important to identify the goals it is hoped to achieve through those subjects and/or activities. Goals need to be set for each of the five areas of the curriculum framework within the context of the student's overall goal.

Activity 1

Individual work

A student's individual goals

Read the following description of the ways in which goals were set for Carl. You will remember from Work session 11 that we learned the following about Carl:

Carl	
Long term aim	employment
Strengths	'good with his hands'
	an interest in cars and motorbikes
Needs	a programme consisting mainly of practical activities
	work experience
	specialist counselling to help him to 'manage' his anger
	'survival' cookery course
	basic budgeting / home management skills
	help to structure his leisure time

This information provided the starting point for a meeting which was held to devise goals for Carl for the first term of his placement. Carl's tutor and his key worker had helped him to prepare for the meeting. It was made clear to Carl that at the end of the meeting he would be required to sign a learning agreement outlining his programme and stating his willingness to participate in it.

The meeting started with a discussion of Carl's long-term aim. Carl agreed that he was hoping to find employment and to live in a flat or bedsit. He stated that he would really like to be a car mechanic.

Carl's tutor felt that his long-term aim was realistic and achievable if Carl was prepared to work at it. The discussion then moved on to an analysis of the skills that Carl would need to develop in order to achieve his long-term goal. The following skills were prioritised for development:

Carl

Skills for development

- those needed to achieve nationally recognised vocational qualifications

- work discipline (punctuality, adherence to rules and regulations, willingness to follow instructions and do as instructed by his employer)

- general employability skills (willingness to accept responsibility, ability to use his own initiative, communication skills, ability to relate to his workmates)

- the ability to control his temper

- strategies to avoid conflict with others

- skills to live independently (basic cooking, washing, ironing, budgeting, cleaning, shopping)

- the ability to use his leisure time constructively.

Once these skills had been identified the meeting moved on to a discussion of Carl's current level of ability and competence in relation to each of the skills that had been prioritised. Information from Carl's previous school, from his social worker and his parents was considered along with the information that staff had gleaned from the time he had spent in the FE unit to help him decide whether or not it would be an appropriate placement for him. Most importantly, Carl was asked for his views as to his ability in relation to the skills listed. From this information it was possible to establish a 'baseline' for the development of Carl's individual programme and the goals it would be appropriate to set for the term.

The following goals were set for the first term and it was decided that Carl's progress would be reviewed at the end of term.

Carl	
Goals (first term)	
Academic	Carl was adamant that he had 'had enough' of school. It was therefore decided that it was inappropriate at this stage to set academic goals for him. It was noted that his school report indicated that he is of above average ability but has specific difficulties with English and maths.
Vocational	to enrol for NVQ level 1 or 2 in motor vehicle engineering at the local college; to attend additional support tutorials in the evenings
Social	to research and participate in at least three new leisure activities; to help Glen (another student) to rebuild his bike
Domestic	to learn to use the washing machine; to learn to iron his own clothes; to cook dinner for himself at the weekends; to learn how to budget for his needs within a set allowance; to be responsible for cleaning his bedroom
Self	to be able to identify what makes him feel angry; to 'walk away' from situations which make him feel angry; to seek help from a member of staff when he feels he is losing control of his temper.

Carl agreed that these goals should be written into a learning agreement which he would sign to confirm his agreement to them and his willingness to work towards their achievement. His tutor and key worker also agreed to sign the learning agreement to indicate that they were aware of Carl's goals and would provide support to help him towards their achievement. His tutor was given responsibility for developing the learning agreement outlining Carl's goals for each aspect of the curriculum, listing teaching and learning strategies that might be useful, and making sure that every member of staff who would come into contact with Carl would be given a copy of the learning agreement.

The meeting ended with a discussion of the roles of the different staff who would be working with Carl. His tutor and his key worker accepted responsibility for informing all staff of the goals that had been agreed with Carl. His tutor was to take responsibility for helping Carl to enrol for his motor vehicle engineering course at the local college and to work with staff at the college to plan a programme of additional support to help him with the theoretical aspects of the course. His key worker was to take responsibility for helping Carl to research and participate in new leisure activities and for helping him to achieve the goals set in relation to domestic skills. All staff were to be aware that Carl might need their support in helping him to control his temper and his key worker agreed to work with Carl to determine what approach staff should take if Carl asked them for help.

Activity 2

Small group work (teachers and care staff)

The right goals?

Discuss the following:

- are the goals set for Carl realistic and relevant to his needs?
- will they enable him to work towards the achievement of his overall aim?
- what changes would you make?

Activity 3

Paired work (a teacher and a member of the care staff)

Defining a student's skill requirements

Analyse the following information about Amy which you were given in Work session 11 and follow the example above for Carl to prioritise the skills she needs to develop if she is to succeed in achieving her overall aim.

Amy	
Long term aim	higher education
Strengths	academically able
	confident and outgoing
Needs	equipment and specialist support to enable her to study the A levels she needs to gain access to higher education
	help to understand the reality of life at university
	help to organise carers to provide the support she requires for her personal needs
	contact with the local coalition of disabled people

Amy
Skills for development

Compare your list with those of the other pairs in the group. Have you prioritised the same skills?

Discuss any differences and come to a consensus as to the skills which are a priority for Amy.

Activity 4

Paired work (a teacher and member of the care staff)

Setting goals

Using the skills you have prioritised for Amy as a starting point, discuss the goals which might be relevant for each of the five areas of the curriculum and list them below.

Amy Goals	
Academic	
Vocational	
Social	
Domestic	
Self	

Present your work to the rest of the group and explain the rationale for the goals you have identified.

Activity 5

Small group work (teachers and care staff)

Learning agreement

Using the examples of Carl and Amy, choose a student with whom you are currently working and work through the separate processes of: devising an overall aim for the student's programme; identifying strengths and needs; prioritising the skills to be learned; writing a learning agreement. Use the following pro forma of a learning agreement to help you.

Learning agreement	
Name of student	
Overall aim	
Goals for the autumn term: (academic year ____)	
Signed (Tutor)	
Signed (Key worker)	
Signed (Student)	

What have you achieved?

You will now have:

- an awareness of the process of setting goals for the five areas of the curriculum within the context of a student's overall aim

- an awareness of the contributions which will be made by the staff who will be working with the student

- developed a learning agreement for a student with whom you are currently working.

Notes

Timetables

(Whole staff)
Once you have determined a student's overall aim, analysed his or her strengths and needs and set goals for the term, the next step is to devise a timetable.

Activity 1

Small groups

From goals to timetable

Study Carl's goals for the term and develop a timetable which builds on the analysis of his needs undertaken in the previous work session. Think carefully about what should be studied within each of the different sessions on the timetable.

Carl	
Goals (first term)	
Vocational	to enrol for NVQ level 1 or 2 motor vehicle engineering
	to attend additional support tutorials in the evenings
Social	to research and participate in at least three new leisure activities
	to help Glen to rebuild his bike
Domestic	to learn to use the washing machine
	to learn to iron his own clothes
	to cook dinner for himself at the weekends
	to learn how to budget for his needs within a set allowance
	to be responsible for cleaning his bedroom
Self	to be able to identify what makes him feel angry to 'walk away' from situations which make him feel angry
	to seek help from a member of staff when he feels he is losing control of his temper

Use the following pro forma to help you.

Student's name:							
Time	Mon	Tues	Weds	Thurs	Fri	Sat	Sun
7–9 a.m.							
9 a.m.–noon							
noon–1 p.m.							
1–4 p.m.							
4–6 p.m.							
6–8 p.m.							
8–10 p.m.							

Activity 2

Paired work (a teacher and a member of the care staff)

From learning agreement to timetable

Using as a starting point the learning agreement you developed in the previous session for a student with whom you are currently working, plan an individual timetable.

Use the following pro forma or devise one that is more appropriate for your establishment.

Student's name:							
Time	Mon	Tues	Weds	Thurs	Fri	Sat	Sun
7–9 a.m.							
9 a.m.–noon							
noon–1 p.m.							
1–4 p.m.							
4–6 p.m.							
6–8 p.m.							
8–10 p.m.							

What have you achieved?

You will now have

- an awareness of the principles underpinning the process of timetabling
- devised a framework for timetabling within your own establishment
- devised a timetable for a student with whom you are currently working.

Notes

Lesson Planning

(Whole staff)

To ensure that students have the best chance of achieving their overall aims it is essential that all the staff who work with them are fully aware of their needs and adopt a consistent approach to their work with them. At the end of the meeting held to develop an individual learning programme for Carl, his tutor and key worker were given the task of liaising with all the staff who will work with Carl to make them aware of his needs and the implications of these for their lesson planning. This task was undertaken by writing a briefing note which was sent to all staff to provide them with information about Carl, his overall aim, his strengths and needs, his goals for the term and the teaching strategies they might find useful. The staff could then set about planning their lessons to meet his needs.

Activity 1

Individual work

Briefing note (to vocational tutor)

Read the following briefing note that Carl's tutor sent to his vocational tutor.

Briefing note

Student's name:

Carl is a new student at the unit. He has not attended school for some time prior to coming to us and is somewhat reluctant to return to education. However, he is keen to find employment and is hoping to live in a flat or bedsit of his own when he leaves the unit. You might find the following information useful when planning lessons which include Carl.

Long term aim	employment
Strengths	'good with his hands' an interest in cars and motorbikes
Needs	a programme consisting of mainly practical activities work experience specialist counselling to help him to 'manage' his anger survival cookery course basic budgeting / home skills help to structure his leisure time
Goals for this term which you can help him work towards	to enrol for NVQ level 1 or 2 in motor vehicle engineering to attend additional support tutorials in the evenings to be able to identify what makes him feel angry to 'walk away' from situations which make him feel angry to seek help from a member of staff when he feels he is losing control of his temper
Teaching strategies that might be successful	Carl learns best through practical activities it is best to demonstrate a task and give verbal instructions avoid giving Carl too much reading and writing make sure that any theoretical work is linked directly to a practical activity – diagrams and 'cartoon type' captions are more effective than long written passages Carl thrives on success – try to plan lessons which will give him opportunities to succeed Carl finds it difficult to concentrate for long periods of time – try to ensure that you plan a variety of activities within a lesson Carl is easily upset by other students – he often claims that they are 'getting at him' because he has difficulty reading – give him opportunities to work on his own but also with another student or small group of students who will be supportive. Allow Carl 'time out' if he feels that he is losing his temper

Activity 2

Paired work (a teacher and a member of the care staff)

Briefing note (to care staff)

Write a briefing note for the care staff who work with Carl.

Activity 3

Paired work (a teacher and a member of the care staff)

Briefing note (to vocational tutor or care staff)

Write a briefing note to inform a vocational tutor or a member of care staff about the student for whom you devised a learning agreement in the previous work session.

Activity 4

Small group work

Consideration of a lesson plan

Consider the following lesson plan which Carl's key worker devised.

Using your leisure time constructively

Students

Glen, Jason, Tracey, Carl, Sonia

Aim

To research leisure activities available in the area

Objectives

At the end of the lesson the students will have:

- discussed their leisure interests

- considered other leisure interests

- identified leisure activities which are available in the area

- chosen leisure activities they would like to try.

Additional specific objectives for Carl:

- to have contributed to group discussion

- to have taken responsibility for operating the television and video recorder

- to have worked with Glen to identify leisure activities advertised in the local paper (specific objectives would also be developed for the other members of the group).

Resources

- local newspaper

- promotional video from local tourist board

- television and video

- leaflets from the local tourist board advertising leisure activities within the area.

Content

- explain purpose of the session to the students

- group discussion to identify current leisure interests

- brainstorm other leisure interests and ways of finding out about leisure activities in the area

- paired work using local papers / leaflets from tourist board to identify leisure activities

- watch short promotional video from tourist board

- every student to identify a new leisure interest they would like to try

- review lesson with students to identify what they have learned

- introduce next lesson – organising a visit to try a new leisure interest.

Evaluation

Reasonably successful session. Students generally participated well. Carl somewhat reluctant to contribute to the discussion at the start of the session (stated he couldn't see the point) but responded positively to my questions about his motorbike. Appears to be quite knowledgeable about grass track events. Carl and Sonia not happy about using newspaper to identify leisure activities even though I didn't ask them to read anything - Carl seemed to be getting quite agitated so I moved on to the video. Everyone responded well to the video – watched with interest, able to answer my questions about what they had seen. Carl knowledgeable about the television and video – seemed to be pleased that I had asked him to operate them – must try to give him some responsibility next session. Sonia worked well with Tracey but soon got bored with the newspapers and leaflets. Carl refused to work with Glen – became abusive. I think it might have been that he was worried about not being able to read the paper and the leaflets rather than not wanting to work with Glen. Will ask him to work with Glen on a practical task next session. He did ask if he could have time out – positive that he recognised that he needed this – returned after five minutes. All students have identified a leisure activity they would like to try.

Now discuss the lesson plan. Consider particularly: how appropriate are the objectives for Carl? How well does the content of the lesson match the aim and objectives set by the key worker?

Activity 5

Paired work

A lesson plan

Following the previous example, plan a lesson for a group of students with whom you are working. Focus particularly on the process of setting individual objectives for each of the students.

Discuss your lesson plan with other members of the group.

What have you achieved?

You will now have:

- an understanding of how to write a briefing note to alert staff to the needs of a student
- an understanding of how to plan lessons to meet the individual needs of students.

Notes

Assessing and Reviewing Progress

(Whole staff)

It is important that students' progress is assessed in relation to their overall aims and the objectives which have been set to help them to achieve these. This is in addition to monitoring progress to meet the requirements of an accrediting or awarding body. Therefore progress must be monitored in each of the five areas of the curriculum, not just a student's vocational/academic programme. It is also essential to review each student's programme in order to assess its effectiveness and to plan any changes which might be necessary.

Carl's end of term review included the following elements:

- a report from his tutors at the local college where he was studying his motor vehicle engineering course

- a report from Carl's tutor at the residential further education unit which incorporated information from all the teachers who worked with him

- a report from Carl's key worker at the residential further education unit which incorporated information from all the care staff who worked with him.

All the staff who worked with Carl were asked to provide information, where possible, about his progress in relation to the goals which had been set at the beginning of term for each area of the extended curriculum. The importance of achieving a realistic assessment of his progress was stressed. Staff were asked to provide evidence of what Carl had learned rather than a description of what he had done over the term.

His tutors at college provided:

- his log book listing the units he had achieved towards his NVQ programme

- a video recording of Carl carrying out a check on a car that had been brought into the workshop for servicing

- a diary they had kept of Carl's behaviour in class.

Activity 1

Small group activity (teachers and care staff)

Assessment evidence

Make a list of the assessment evidence that other people who work with Carl might have presented, e.g.:

- care staff
- tutor
- parents
- other students.

Activity 2

Individual activity

A summary report

Read the summary report prepared by Carl's tutor. It was compiled from the information provided by all the staff who had worked with Carl during the term.

End of term review	
Student	Carl Smith
Personal tutor	Richard Green
Key worker	Paul Taylor
Date	11 December 1997

Summary

After a 'rocky' start to the term when Carl found it difficult to cope with the demands of his programme, he has now settled into the unit and is beginning to make progress in each area of the extended curriculum. Staff have assessed his progress in relation to the goals we set at the beginning of term. (Their assessment records will be available for you to look at in the meeting.)

End of term review (continued)

Vocational

Carl has achieved 3 units towards NVQ level 1. He has attended 8 (out of a possible 15) support tutorials. Initially he refused to attend the tutorials but has attended regularly for the past four weeks. He now recognises that the tutorials help him with his work at college. His tutor at college provides us with the handouts and worksheets he will be using in a lesson one week before and we use the tutorial to make sure Carl can read them. Carl now recognises most of the technical words he has used so far – he has not found it difficult to learn these. He is still having difficulty with the written work. His tutors have reduced the amount of written work he has to do by creating worksheets with boxes which contain statements which he can tick or cross. In tutorials we are practising completing worksheets. Carl knows the answers to the questions but has difficulty writing these. He has difficulty spelling some of the words and his handwriting is rather large. This makes it difficult for him to fit his writing into the space available. We are now concentrating on helping him to spell the words he needs for his course and practising writing the words within small boxes.

Social

Carl has researched the leisure activities available in the area. He decided to try mountain biking, fishing and tenpin bowling. So far, he has been tenpin bowling with a small group of students from the unit and has planned a trip to Derbyshire for himself and Glen on their mountain bikes. Jason is planning a fishing trip and Carl has agreed to accompany him. Carl has worked well with Glen. He seems to have gained confidence from the fact that he has been able to teach Glen how to go about rebuilding his bike. Carl has experienced some difficulties in working with other members of the group. He lacks confidence and feels that they are 'getting at him'. He finds it particularly difficult to work with Sonia. Carl still spends a lot of time in his room on his own. He needs a lot of persuading to join the rest of the students on visits. He has gone to the pub with them on a couple of occasions over the last few weeks but came back early last week. He has difficulty initiating and sustaining conversations, particularly with people he does not know.

End of term review (continued)

Domestic

Carl has made slow progress in this area. He has learned to use the two programmes he needs on the washing machine but needs constant prompting to do his washing. He refuses to do any ironing. He has not cleaned his bedroom since the beginning of term - he says it's not his job – 'that's what the cleaner gets paid for'. He has cooked dinner for himself at the weekend. He has made simple meals such as beans on toast and egg and chips. He is quite competent practically but reluctant to clean up after he has finished and unwilling to try anything new. Carl has responded well to being given a weekly allowance for his leisure activities. He has been careful not to overspend and has managed to save a small amount towards a new cycling T-shirt.

Self

Carl has made sound progress in this area of the extended curriculum. He now recognises that it is other people that make him feel angry and he has learned to walk away from situations in which he feels he is losing control of his temper. For example, there have been occasions when he and Glen have argued but Carl has not lost his temper and has taken himself off to his room to 'cool down'. Carl has found it more difficult to relate to other students in his group at college. He feels that they think he is 'thick' and that they talk about him behind his back. He spends most of his breaktimes on his own – he says he is happier doing this because he might be tempted to punch someone if he felt they were getting at him. It is positive that on a number of occasions Carl has sought help from his support worker at college when he has felt himself losing control.

Activity 3

Paired activity (a teacher and a member of the care staff)

Analysing the report

What does the report tell you about Carl's progress? What information do you think is missing? How would you alter the way in which the information has been presented?

Once all the assessment information had been received, Carl's tutor and his key worker helped him to review the progress he had made during the term. They went through the evidence submitted by the different staff, and helped him to prepare for the review meeting which was to be held to discuss his progress. Carl was worried that he might find it difficult to express his views in the meeting. His tutor and key worker suggested that he might prefer to record his views on an audio tape which could be played at the meeting. Carl agreed to this and used one of his support tutorials to produce the tape.

Activity 4

Small group activity

How students can contribute to their own reviews

How else might Carl have presented his views of his progress at his review meeting?

Carl's review meeting

The review meeting which was held at the end of the first term was attended by Carl, his key worker and tutor from the FE unit, his careers officer and his mother. Prior to the meeting, everyone had been sent a copy of Carl's end of term report. All the evidence that had been used to compile the report was taken to the meeting for people to examine. The deputy principal welcomed everyone to the meeting and explained that the purpose was to review the progress that Carl had made in relation to his overall aim and the goals that had been set for the first term, and to consider any changes that needed to be made to his individual programme.

Carl's tutor summarised the report he had sent to everyone prior to the meeting. Mrs Smith was asked if she would like to present any further information about Carl's progress. Carl chose to play the audio tape he had prepared to explain his thoughts about his programme and the progress he had made.

Carl's tutor then outlined what, in his view, were the main issues for consideration. These were:

- Carl seems to be making sound progress in his vocational studies. Staff at college feel that he should continue with the course. They expect him to be able to achieve NVQ level 2 (probably within two years). He appears to be particularly competent in practical sessions.

- Carl's improved attendance at his support tutorials is beginning to have an impact on his ability to 'keep up' with the theoretical aspects of his programme. The methods used to help him with his reading, spelling and handwriting are working well. However, he will need to make a commitment to attending these sessions each week.

- Some progress has been made in relation to his social skills. Carl has worked positively with Glen and both have gained from this. Carl has accepted that he needs to 'work at' his relationship with others, particularly people he does not know well. He prefers his own company to that of other people but understands that this is mainly because he lacks confidence when he is with a group of people. Careful thought will need to be given to planning activities which enable Carl to work with other students.

- Carl's lack of progress in domestic skills. Carl claims that the care staff are always 'nagging' him to do his washing and ironing and to clean his room. He says this makes him more determined not to do it. He knows that he will need to improve his skills if he wants to move to his own flat or bedsit. This is an area of the curriculum which will need to be rethought carefully.

- Perhaps the most pleasing aspect of Carl's progress has been his ability to control his temper. He has sought help when necessary and has avoided trouble for most of the term. Allowing him 'time out' has proved very successful. We will need to think of ways of helping Carl to cope with situations as they happen without having to rely on 'time out'.

Throughout the meeting care was taken to praise Carl for the progress he had made and to avoid making him feel that his lack of progress in domestic skills was entirely his fault. The discussion focused on trying to establish the reasons for the lack of progress rather than blaming Carl.

At the end of the meeting Carl confirmed that he agreed with what his tutor had said and stated that he was still keen to find employment as a motor mechanic and to live independently in a flat or bedsit.

The meeting then focused on setting new goals for Carl for the next term.

Activity 5

Small group discussion

Reviewing and adapting

- What strategies have helped Carl to succeed?
- What factors might have contributed to his lack of progress in domestic skills?
- What lessons do staff working with Carl need to learn?
- What changes need to be made to Carl's programme?
- Is the overall aim still appropriate?
- What goals would you set for the next term?

- What information should be given to the staff who work with Carl?

- What strategies would you recommend that they use in their work with him?

- What feedback should be given to Carl?

What have you achieved?

You will now have:

- an awareness of the ways in which evidence of progress can be presented

- an understanding of how a student's progress can be monitored in relation to his/her overall aim and the individual goals that were set

- an awareness of who needs to be involved in reviewing a student's progress

- an awareness of the process of reviewing and evaluating a student's individual programme

- an awareness of the process of setting new goals.

Notes

Summary

When you have completed all the activities, you will have created a unique curriculum framework for your establishment, and individual learning programmes for all the students. That is a major achievement. You should make sure that you celebrate the achievement, as well as implementing the new curriculum for the benefit of the students.

Matthew Griffiths and Carol Tennyson would like to hear from establishments who successfully complete the programme, and would be particularly interested in receiving information about the ways in which staff teams worked together to bring about change.

Bibliography

Further Education Funding Council (1997) *Good Practice: provision for students with learning difficulties and/or disabilities.* Coventry: FEFC.

Further Education Unit/MENCAP (1994) *Learning for Life: a pack to support adults who have profound intellectual and multiple physical disabilities.* London: FEU.

Griffiths, M. (1994) *Transition to Adulthood.* London: David Fulton Publishers.

Learning Difficulties and/or Disabilities Committee to the Further Education Funding Council (1996) *Inclusive Learning.* London: HMSO.

Notes

Notes

Notes

Notes

Notes

Notes

Notes